THE SUN ALSO RISES

Ernest Hemingway

Spark Publishing
A Division of Barnes & Noble
120 Fifth Avenue
New York, NY 10011
www.sparknotes.com

ISBN-13: 978-1-5866-3385-1
ISBN-10: 1-5866-3385-6

Please submit changes or report errors to www.sparknotes.com/errors.

Printed and bound in the United States

9 10

Introduction: Stopping to Buy SparkNotes on a Snowy Evening

Whose words these are you *think* you know.
Your paper's due tomorrow, though;
We're glad to see you stopping here
To get some help before you go.

Lost your course? You'll find it here.
Face tests and essays without fear.
Between the words, good grades at stake:
Get great results throughout the year.

Once school bells caused your heart to quake
As teachers circled each mistake.
Use SparkNotes and no longer weep,
Ace every single test you take.

Yes, books are lovely, dark, and deep,
But only what you grasp you keep,
With hours to go before you sleep,
With hours to go before you sleep.

CONTENTS

CONTEXT   I

PLOT OVERVIEW   3

CHARACTER LIST   6

ANALYSIS OF MAJOR CHARACTERS   10

THEMES, MOTIFS & SYMBOLS   13
    THE AIMLESSNESS OF THE LOST GENERATION   13
    MALE INSECURITY   13
    THE DESTRUCTIVENESS OF SEX   14
    THE FAILURE OF COMMUNICATION   15
    EXCESSIVE DRINKING   15
    FALSE FRIENDSHIPS   15
    BULLFIGHTING   16

SUMMARY & ANALYSIS   18
    A NOTE ON THE EPIGRAPH   18
    CHAPTERS I–II   18
    CHAPTERS III–IV   21
    CHAPTERS V–VII   24
    CHAPTERS VIII–X   27
    CHAPTERS XI–XII   29
    CHAPTERS XIII–XIV   32
    CHAPTER XV   35
    CHAPTER XVI   37
    CHAPTER XVII   39
    CHAPTERS XVIII–XIX   41

IMPORTANT QUOTATIONS EXPLAINED   45

KEY FACTS   48

STUDY QUESTIONS & ESSAY TOPICS   50

REVIEW & RESOURCES   53

CONTEXT

ERNEST MILLER HEMINGWAY WAS BORN on July 21, 1899, in Oak Park, Illinois, a conservative upper-middle-class suburb of Chicago. He graduated from high school in 1917 and worked as a reporter for the *Kansas City Star.* Hemingway sailed to Europe in May 1918 to serve as a volunteer ambulance driver for the Italian Red Cross during World War I. Within weeks, he suffered a serious injury from fragments of an exploding mortar shell on the Italian front. He recovered in a hospital in Milan, where he had a romantic relationship with a nurse, Agnes von Kurowsky. This incident provided the inspiration for his novel *A Farewell to Arms,* published in 1929.

When the nineteen-year-old Hemingway returned home in 1919, his parents did not understand the psychological trauma he had suffered during the war, and they pestered him to get a job or go to college. His short story "Soldier's Home" draws on his difficulties in coping with his parents' and friends' romanticized ideals of war.

Hemingway eventually began working for the *Toronto Star Weekly.* He married his first wife, Hadley Richardson, in 1921. He became the European correspondent for the *Toronto Daily Star* and moved to Paris with his wife in December 1921. There, Hemingway became friends with the poet Ezra Pound, the writer Gertrude Stein, the artists Joan Miró and Pablo Picasso, and other individuals belonging to the group of prominent expatriate writers and artists living in postwar Paris. Hemingway's reputation began to grow both as a journalist and as an author of fiction. His novel *The Sun Also Rises,* published in 1926, established him as one of the preeminent writers of his day.

The Sun Also Rises portrays the lives of the members of the so-called Lost Generation, the group of men and women whose early adulthood was consumed by World War I. This horrific conflict, referred to as the Great War, set new standards for death and immorality in war. It shattered many people's beliefs in traditional values of love, faith, and manhood. Without these long-held notions to rely on, members of the generation that fought and worked in the war suffered great moral and psychological aimlessness. The futile search for meaning in the wake of the Great War shapes *The Sun*

Also Rises. Although the characters rarely mention the war directly, its effects haunt everything they do and say.

Amid the increasing literary success that followed the publication of *The Sun Also Rises,* Hemingway's marriage began to fall apart, and he divorced Richardson in 1927. He quickly remarried, to a fashion reporter named Pauline Pfeiffer. In 1928, they moved to Key West, Florida, where they lived for over a decade. Hemingway's life, however, was far from rosy. His father, Clarence Hemingway, committed suicide in 1928 after developing serious health and financial problems, and Hemingway engaged in an affair with a woman named Martha Gelhorn, which led to his divorce from Pfeiffer. He married Gelhorn in 1940.

In 1937, Hemingway traveled to Spain to cover the Spanish Civil War for the North American Newspaper Alliance. His novel *For Whom the Bell Tolls,* based on his experiences in Spain, was published in 1940, after he moved to Havana, Cuba, with Gelhorn. The book became an instant success, but he did not publish another novel for ten years. Meanwhile, he and Gelhorn divorced, and Hemingway married Mary Welsh, his fourth and last wife. Hemingway won the Pulitzer Prize in 1953 for his phenomenally successful *The Old Man and the Sea* and the Nobel Prize in Literature in 1954.

Deteriorating health began to plague Hemingway. His heavy drinking increased his health problems, and he began to suffer from wild mood swings. In 1960, Hemingway and Welsh moved to Ketchum, Idaho. Not long afterward, he entered the Mayo Clinic to undergo treatment for severe depression. His depression worsened in 1961, and on July 2 of that year, Hemingway woke early in the morning and committed suicide by shooting himself in the head.

Hemingway's style differs distinctively from that of writers before him, and his work helped shape both the British and American literature that followed it. His prose is extremely spare, succinct, and seemingly very direct, although his speakers tend to give the impression that they are leaving a tremendous amount unsaid. Modern prose fiction continues to be heavily influenced by Hemingway's technique in this regard. His body of work continues to be considered among the most important in the development of twentieth-century literature.

PLOT OVERVIEW

THE SUN ALSO RISES opens with the narrator, Jake Barnes, delivering a brief biographical sketch of his friend, Robert Cohn. Jake is a veteran of World War I who now works as a journalist in Paris. Cohn is also an American expatriate, although not a war veteran. He is a rich Jewish writer who lives in Paris with his forceful and controlling girlfriend, Frances Clyne. Cohn has become restless of late, and he comes to Jake's office one afternoon to try to convince Jake to go with him to South America. Jake refuses, and he takes pains to get rid of Cohn. That night at a dance club, Jake runs into Lady Brett Ashley, a divorced socialite and the love of Jake's life. Brett is a free-spirited and independent woman, but she can be very selfish at times. She and Jake met in England during World War I, when Brett treated Jake for a war wound. During Jake and Brett's conversation, it is subtly implied that Jake's injury rendered him impotent. Although Brett loves Jake, she hints that she is unwilling to give up sex, and that for this reason she will not commit to a relationship with him.

The next morning, Jake and Cohn have lunch. Cohn is quite taken with Brett, and he gets angry when Jake tells him that Brett plans to marry Mike Campbell, a heavy-drinking Scottish war veteran. That afternoon, Brett stands Jake up. That night, however, she arrives unexpectedly at his apartment with Count Mippipopolous, a rich Greek expatriate. After sending the count out for champagne, Brett tells Jake that she is leaving for San Sebastian, in Spain, saying it will be easier on both of them to be apart.

Several weeks later, while Brett and Cohn are both traveling outside of Paris, one of Jake's friends, a fellow American war veteran named Bill Gorton, arrives in Paris. Bill and Jake make plans to leave for Spain to do some fishing and later attend the fiesta at Pamplona. Jake makes plans to meet Cohn on the way to Pamplona. Jake runs into Brett, who has returned from San Sebastian; with her is Mike, her fiancé. They ask if they may join Jake in Spain, and he politely responds that they may. When Mike leaves for a moment, Brett reveals to Jake that she and Cohn were in San Sebastian together.

Bill and Jake take a train from Paris to Bayonne, in the south of France, where they meet Cohn. The three men travel together into Spain, to Pamplona. They plan on meeting Brett and Mike that night, but the couple does not show up. Bill and Jake decide to leave for a small town called Burguete to fish, but Cohn chooses to stay and wait for Brett. Bill and Jake travel to the Spanish countryside and check into a small, rural inn. They spend five pleasant days fishing, drinking, and playing cards. Eventually, Jake receives a letter from Mike. He writes that he and Brett will be arriving in Pamplona shortly. Jake and Bill leave on a bus that afternoon to meet the couple. After arriving in Pamplona, Jake and Bill check into a hotel owned by Montoya, a Spanish bullfighting expert who likes Jake for his earnest interest in the sport. Jake and Bill meet up with Brett, Mike, and Cohn, and the whole group goes to watch the bulls being unloaded in preparation for the bullfights during the fiesta. Mike mocks Cohn harshly for following Brett around when he is not wanted.

After a few more days of preparation, the fiesta begins. The city is consumed with dancing, drinking, and general debauchery. The highlight of the first day is the first bullfight, at which Pedro Romero, a nineteen-year-old prodigy, distinguishes himself above all the other bullfighters. Despite its violence, Brett cannot take her eyes off the bullfight, or Romero. A few days later, Jake and his friends are at the hotel dining room, and Brett notices Romero at a nearby table. She persuades Jake to introduce her to him. Mike again verbally abuses Cohn, and they almost come to blows before Jake defuses the situation. Later that night, Brett asks Jake to help her find Romero, with whom she says she has fallen in love. Jake agrees to help, and Brett and Romero spend the night together.

Jake then meets up with Mike and Bill, who are both extremely drunk. Cohn soon arrives, demanding to know where Brett is. After an exchange of insults, Cohn attacks Mike and Jake, knocking them both out. When Jake returns to the hotel, he finds Cohn lying face down on his bed and crying. Cohn begs Jake's forgiveness, and Jake reluctantly grants it. The next day, Jake learns from Bill and Mike that the night before Cohn also beat up Romero when he discovered the bullfighter with Brett; Cohn later begged Romero to shake hands with him, but Romero refused.

At the bullfight that afternoon, Romero fights brilliantly, dazzling the crowd by killing a bull that had gored a man to death in the streets. Afterward, he cuts the bull's ear off and gives it to Brett.

After this final bullfight, Romero and Brett leave for Madrid together. Cohn has left that morning, so only Bill, Mike, and Jake remain as the fiesta draws to a close.

The next day, the three remaining men rent a car and drive out of Spain to Bayonne and then go their separate ways. Jake heads back into Spain to San Sebastian, where he plans to spend several quiet days relaxing. He receives a telegram from Brett, however, asking him to come meet her in Madrid. He complies, and boards an overnight train that same day. Jake finds Brett alone in a Madrid hotel room. She has broken with Romero, fearing that she would ruin him and his career. She announces that she now wants to return to Mike. Jake books tickets for them to leave Madrid. As they ride in a taxi through the Spanish capital, Brett laments that she and Jake could have had a wonderful time together. Jake responds, "Yes, isn't it pretty to think so?"

CHARACTER LIST

CHARACTER LIST

Jake Barnes The narrator and protagonist of the novel. Jake is an American veteran of World War I working as a journalist in Paris, where he and his friends engage in an endless round of drinking and parties. Although Jake is the most stable of his friends, he struggles with anguish over his love for Lady Brett Ashley, his impotence, and the moral vacuum that resulted from the war. Jake positions himself as an observer, generally using his insight and intelligence to describe only those around him, rarely speaking directly about himself. However, in describing the events and people he sees, Jake implicitly reveals much about his own thoughts and feelings.

Lady Brett Ashley A beautiful British socialite who drinks heavily. As the novel begins, Brett is separated from her husband and awaiting a divorce. Though she loves Jake, she is unwilling to commit to a relationship with him because it will mean giving up sex. Indeed, she is unwilling to commit fully to any of the many men who become infatuated with her, though she has affairs with a number of them. However, she does not seem to draw much happiness from her independence. Her life, like the lives of many in her generation, is aimless and unfulfilling.

Robert Cohn A wealthy American writer living in Paris. Though he is an expatriate like many of his acquaintances, Cohn stands apart because he had no direct experience of World War I and because he is Jewish. He holds on to the romantic prewar ideals of love and fair play, yet, against the backdrop of the devastating legacy of World War I, these values seem tragically absurd. As a Jew and a nonveteran, Cohn is a convenient target for the cruel and petty antagonism of Jake and his friends.

Bill Gorton Like Jake, a heavy-drinking war veteran, though not an expatriate. Bill uses humor to deal with the emotional and psychological fallout of World War I. He and Jake, as American veterans, share a strong bond, and their friendship is one of the few genuine emotional connections in the novel. However, Bill is not immune to the petty cruelty that characterizes Jake and Jake's circle of friends.

Mike Campbell A constantly drunk, bankrupt Scottish war veteran. Mike has a terrible temper, which most often manifests itself during his extremely frequent bouts of drunkenness. He has a great deal of trouble coping with Brett's sexual promiscuity, which provokes outbreaks of self-pity and anger in him, and seems insecure about her infidelity as well as his lack of money.

Pedro Romero A beautiful, nineteen-year-old bullfighter. Romero's talents in the ring charm both aficionados and newcomers to the sport alike. He serves as a foil (a character whose attitudes or emotions contrast with, and thereby accentuate, those of another character) for Jake and his friends in that he carries himself with dignity and confidence at all times. Moreover, his passion for bullfighting gives his life meaning and purpose. In a world of amorality and corrupted masculinity, Romero remains a figure of honesty, purity, and strength.

Montoya The owner of a Pamplona inn and a bullfighting expert. Montoya sees bullfighting as something sacred, and he respects and admires Jake for his genuine enthusiasm about it. Montoya takes a paternal interest in the gifted young bullfighter Pedro Romero and seeks to protect him from the corrupting influences of tourists and fame.

Frances Clyne Cohn's girlfriend at the beginning of the novel. A manipulative status-seeker, Frances was highly domineering early in their relationship and persuaded Cohn to move to Paris. As her looks begin to fade, she becomes increasingly possessive and jealous.

Count Mippipopolous A wealthy Greek count and a veteran of seven wars and four revolutions. Count Mippipopolous becomes infatuated with Brett, but, unlike most of Brett's lovers, he does not subject her to jealous, controlling behavior. Amid the careless, amoral pleasure-seeking crowd that constitutes Jake's social circle, the count stands out as a stable, sane person. Like Pedro Romero, he serves as a foil for Jake and his friends.

Wilson-Harris A British war veteran whom Jake and Bill befriend while fishing in Spain. The three men share a profound common bond, having all experienced the horrors of World War I, as well as the intimacy that soldiers develop. Harris, as Jake and Bill call him, is a kind, friendly person who greatly values the brief time he spends with Jake and Bill.

Georgette A beautiful but somewhat thick-witted prostitute whom Jake picks up and takes to dinner. Jake quickly grows bored of their superficial conversation and abandons her in a club to be with Brett.

Belmonte A bullfighter who fights on the same day as Pedro Romero. In his early days, Belmonte was a great and popular bullfighter. But when he came out of retirement to fight again, he found he could never live up to the legends that had grown around him. Hence, he is bitter and dejected. He seems to symbolize the entire Lost Generation in that he feels out of place and purposeless in his later adult life.

Harvey Stone A drunken expatriate gambler who is perpetually out of money. Harvey is intelligent and well read, yet he cannot escape his demons of excessive drinking and gambling. Like many of Jake's friends, he is prone to petty cruelty toward Cohn.

ANALYSIS OF MAJOR CHARACTERS

JAKE BARNES

The key events in the formation of Jake's character occur long before the novel's action begins. As a soldier in World War I, Jake is wounded. Although he does not say so directly, there are numerous moments in the novel when he implies that, as a result of his injury, he has lost the ability to have sex. Jake's narration is characterized by subtlety and implication. He prefers to hint at things rather than state them outright, especially when they concern the war or his injury. Early in the novel, for example one must read the text very closely to grasp the true nature of Jake's wound; it is only later, when Jake goes fishing with Bill, that he speaks more openly about his impotence.

Jake's physical malady has profound psychological consequences. He seems quite insecure about his masculinity. The fact that Brett, the love of his life, refuses to enter into a relationship with him compounds this problem. Jake, with typical subtlety, suggests that she does not want to because it would mean giving up sexual intercourse. Jake's hostility toward Robert Cohn is perhaps rooted in his own feelings of inadequacy. In many ways, Jake is a typical member of what poet Gertrude Stein called the "lost generation," the generation of men and women whose experiences in World War I undermined their belief in justice, morality, manhood, and love. Without these ideals to rely on, the Lost Generation lived an aimless, immoral existence, devoid of true emotion and characterized by casual interpersonal cruelty. Part of Jake's character represents the Lost Generation and its unfortunate position: he wanders through Paris, going from bar to bar and drinking heavily at each, his life filled with purposeless debauchery. He demonstrates the capacity to be extremely cruel, especially toward Cohn. His insecurities about his masculinity are typical of the anxieties that many members of the Lost Generation felt.

Yet, in some important ways, Jake differs from those around him. He seems aware of the fruitlessness of the Lost Generation's way of life. He tells Cohn in Chapter II: "You can't get away from yourself by moving from one place to another." Moreover, he recognizes the frequent cruelty of the behavior in which he and his friends engage. Most important, perhaps, he acknowledges, if only indirectly, the pain that his war injury and his unrequited love for Brett cause him. However, though Jake does perceive the problems in his life, he seems either unwilling or unable to remedy them. Though he understands the dilemma of the Lost Generation, he remains trapped within it.

LADY BRETT ASHLEY

Brett is a strong, largely independent woman. She exerts great power over the men around her, as her beauty and charisma seem to charm everyone she meets. Moreover, she refuses to commit to any one man, preferring ultimate independence. However, her independence does not make her happy. She frequently complains to Jake about how miserable she is—her life, she claims, is aimless and unsatisfying. Her wandering from relationship to relationship parallels Jake and his friends' wandering from bar to bar. Although she will not commit to any one man, she seems uncomfortable being by herself. As Jake remarks, "She can't go anywhere alone."

Indeed, there are several misogynist strains in Hemingway's representation of Brett. For instance, she disrupts relationships between men with her very presence. It seems that, in Hemingway's view, a liberated woman is necessarily a corrupting, dangerous force for men. Brett represents a threat to Pedro Romero and his career—she believes that her own strength and independence will eventually spoil Romero's strength and independence. Because she does not conform to traditional feminine behavior, she is a danger to him.

As with Jake and his male friends, World War I seems to have played an essential part in the formation of Brett's character. During the war, Brett's true love died of dysentery. Her subsequent aimlessness, especially with regard to men, can be interpreted as a futile, subconscious search for this original love. Brett's personal search is perhaps symbolic of the entire Lost Generation's search for the shattered prewar values of love and romance.

ROBERT COHN

Cohn has spent his entire life feeling like an outsider because he is Jewish. While at Princeton, he took up boxing to combat his feelings of shyness and inferiority. Although his confidence has grown with his literary success, his anxiety about being different or considered not good enough persists. These feelings of otherness and inadequacy may explain his irrational attachment to Brett—he is so terrified of rejection that, when it happens, he refuses to accept it.

The individuals with whom Cohn travels to Spain only compound his insecurities. Not only is he the only Jew among them, but he is also the only nonveteran. Jake and his friends seize on these differences and take out their own personal insecurities on Cohn. It is important to note that Cohn's behavior toward Brett is ultimately not very different from that of most of the men in the novel. They all want to possess her in ways that she resists. But Cohn's attempts to win Brett are so clumsy and foolish that they provide an easy target for mockery.

Cohn adheres to an outdated, prewar value system of honor and romance. He fights only within the confines of the gym until his rage and frustration make him lash out at Romero and Jake. He plays hard at tennis, but if he loses he accepts defeat gracefully. Furthermore, he cannot believe that his affair with Brett has no emotional value. Hence, he acts as a foil for Jake and the other veterans in the novel; unlike them, he holds onto traditional values and beliefs, likely because he never experienced World War I firsthand.

Sadly, Cohn's value system has no place in the postwar world, and Cohn cannot sustain it. His tearful request that Romero shake his hand after Cohn has beaten him up is an absurd attempt to restore the validity of an antiquated code of conduct. His flight from Pamplona is symbolic of the failure of traditional values in the postwar world.

THEMES, MOTIFS & SYMBOLS

THEMES

Themes are the fundamental and often universal ideas explored in a literary work.

THE AIMLESSNESS OF THE LOST GENERATION

World War I undercut traditional notions of morality, faith, and justice. No longer able to rely on the traditional beliefs that gave life meaning, the men and women who experienced the war became psychologically and morally lost, and they wandered aimlessly in a world that appeared meaningless. Jake, Brett, and their acquaintances give dramatic life to this situation. Because they no longer believe in anything, their lives are empty. They fill their time with inconsequential and escapist activities, such as drinking, dancing, and debauchery.

It is important to note that Hemingway never explicitly states that Jake and his friends' lives are aimless, or that this aimlessness is a result of the war. Instead, he implies these ideas through his portrayal of the characters' emotional and mental lives. These stand in stark contrast to the characters' surface actions. Jake and his friends' constant carousing does not make them happy. Very often, their merrymaking is joyless and driven by alcohol. At best, it allows them not to think about their inner lives or about the war. Although they spend nearly all of their time partying in one way or another, they remain sorrowful or unfulfilled. Hence, their drinking and dancing is just a futile distraction, a purposeless activity characteristic of a wandering, aimless life.

MALE INSECURITY

World War I forced a radical reevaluation of what it meant to be masculine. The prewar ideal of the brave, stoic soldier had little relevance in the context of brutal trench warfare that characterized the war. Soldiers were forced to sit huddled together as the enemy bombarded them. Survival depended far more upon luck than upon bravery. Traditional notions of what it meant to be a man were thus undermined by the realities of the war. Jake embodies these cultural changes. The war renders his manhood (that is, his penis) useless because of injury. He carries the burden of feeling that he is "less of a man" than he was before. He cannot escape a nagging sense of inadequacy, which is only compounded by Brett's refusal to enter into a relationship with him.

While Jake's condition is the most explicit example of weakened masculinity in the novel, it is certainly not the only one. All of the veterans feel insecure in their manhood. Again, Hemingway does not state this fact directly, but rather shows it in the way Jake and his veteran friends react to Cohn. They target Cohn in particular for abuse when they see him engaging in "unmanly" behavior such as following Brett around. They cope with their fears of being weak and unmasculine by criticizing the weakness they see in him. Hemingway further presents this theme in his portrayal of Brett. In many ways, she is more "manly" than the men in the book. She refers to herself as a "chap," she has a short, masculine haircut and a masculine name, and she is strong and independent. Thus, she embodies traditionally masculine characteristics, while Jake, Mike, and Bill are to varying degrees uncertain of their masculinity.

THE DESTRUCTIVENESS OF SEX

Sex is a powerful and destructive force in *The Sun Also Rises*. Sexual jealousy, for example, leads Cohn to violate his code of ethics and attack Jake, Mike, and Romero. Furthermore, the desire for sex prevents Brett from entering into a relationship with Jake, although she loves him. Hence, sex undermines both Cohn's honor and Jake and Brett's love. Brett is closely associated with the negative consequences of sex. She is a liberated woman, having sex with multiple men and feeling no compulsion to commit to any of them. Her carefree sexuality makes Jake and Mike miserable and drives Cohn to acts of violence. In Brett, Hemingway may be expressing his own anxieties about strong, sexually independent women.

MOTIFS

Motifs are recurring structures, contrasts, or literary devices that can help to develop and inform the text's major themes.

THE FAILURE OF COMMUNICATION

The conversations among Jake and his friends are rarely direct or honest. They hide true feelings behind a mask of civility. Although the legacy of the war torments them all, they are unable to communicate this torment. They can talk about the war only in an excessively humorous or painfully trite fashion. An example of the latter occurs when Georgette and Jake have dinner, and Jake narrates that they would probably have gone on to agree that the war "would have been better avoided" if they were not fortunately interrupted. The moments of honest, genuine communication generally arise only when the characters are feeling their worst. Consequently, only very dark feelings are expressed. When Brett torments Jake especially harshly, for instance, he expresses his unhappiness with her and their situation. Similarly, when Mike is hopelessly drunk, he tells Cohn how much his presence disgusts him. Expressions of true affection, on the other hand, are limited almost exclusively to Jake and Bill's fishing trip.

EXCESSIVE DRINKING

Nearly all of Jake's friends are alcoholics. Wherever they happen to be, they drink, usually to excess. Often, their drinking provides a way of escaping reality. Drunkenness allows Jake and his acquaintances to endure lives severely lacking in affection and purpose. Hemingway clearly portrays the drawbacks to this excessive drinking. Alcohol frequently brings out the worst in the characters, particularly Mike. He shows himself to be a nasty, violent man when he is intoxicated. More subtly, Hemingway also implies that drunkenness only worsens the mental and emotional turmoil that plagues Jake and his friends. Being drunk allows them to avoid confronting their problems by providing them with a way to avoid thinking about them. However, drinking is not exclusively portrayed in a negative light. In the context of Jake and Bill's fishing trip, for instance, it can be a relaxing, friendship-building, even healthy activity.

FALSE FRIENDSHIPS

False friendships relate closely to failed communication. Many of the friendships in the novel have no basis in affection. For instance, Jake meets a bicycle team manager, and the two have a drink together. They enjoy a friendly conversation and make plans to meet the next morning. Jake, however, sleeps through their meeting, having no regard for the fact that he will never see the man again. Jake and Cohn demonstrate another, still darker type of false friendship. Although Cohn genuinely likes Jake, Jake must often mask outright antagonism toward Cohn, an antagonism that increases dramatically along with Jake's unspoken jealousy of Cohn over his affair with Brett. At one point, he even claims to hate Cohn. This inability to form genuine connections with other people is an aspect of the aimless wandering that characterizes Jake's existence. Jake and his friends wander socially as well as geographically. Ironically, Hemingway suggests that in the context of war it was easier to form connections with other people. In peacetime it proves far more difficult for these characters to do so.

SYMBOLS

Symbols are objects, characters, figures, or colors used to represent abstract ideas or concepts.

BULLFIGHTING

The bullfighting episodes in *The Sun Also Rises* are rich in symbolic possibilities. The multiple possible interpretations of these passages speak to the depth and complexity of the text. For example, nearly every episode involving bulls or bullfighting parallels an episode that either has occurred, or will soon occur, among Jake and his friends. The killing of the steer by the bull at the start of the fiesta, for instance, may prefigure Mike's assault on Cohn. Alternatively, we can read this incident as prefiguring Brett's destruction of Cohn and his values. Furthermore, the bullfighting episodes nearly always function from two symbolic viewpoints: Jake's perspective and the perspective of postwar society. For instance, we can interpret the figure of Belmonte from the point of view of Jake and his friends. Just as Cohn, Mike, and Jake all once commanded Brett's affection, so too did Belmonte once command the affection of the crowd, which now discards him for Romero. In a larger context, Belmonte can symbolize the entire Lost Generation, whose moment seems to have passed. On still another level, Hemingway uses bullfighting to develop the theme of the destructiveness of sex. The language Hemingway employs to describe Romero's bullfighting is almost always sexual, and his killing of the bull takes the form of a seduction. This symbolic equation of sex and violence further links sexuality to danger and destruction. It is important to note that the distinctions between these interpretations are not hard and fast. Rather, levels of meaning in *The Sun Also Rises* flow together and complement one another.

SUMMARY & ANALYSIS

A NOTE ON THE EPIGRAPH

Gertrude Stein was an avant-garde American poet at the center of a group of painters and expatriate writers living in Paris after World War I. Among those in her circle were the artist Pablo Picasso and the writers Sherwood Anderson and Ernest Hemingway. Stein named the generation that came of age during World War I the "lost generation." The world quickly adopted the phrase as the most accurate description of the generation that passed through the threshold of adulthood at this time—working, fighting, or dying in the war. The horrific conflict shattered this generation's faith in traditional values such as love, bravery, manhood, and woman-hood. Without these values, the members of this generation found their existence aimless, meaningless, and unfulfilling. It is these men and women that Hemingway portrays in *The Sun Also Rises*.

Before the novel opens, Hemingway quotes Stein and a biblical passage from Ecclesiastes. The passage contrasts the transient nature of human generations with the eternal survival of nature: the world endures, and the sun continues to rise and set despite the inev-itable passage of each human generation into death. Hemingway's juxtaposition of the two epigraphs produces an ambivalent tone. On the one hand, there is hope, because there will be a new genera-tion after the aimless generation that populates *The Sun Also Rises*. On the other hand, there is bitter irony, since every generation is lost, in the sense that each generation will eventually die.

CHAPTERS I–II

SUMMARY: CHAPTER I

> [Cohn] learned [boxing] painfully and thoroughly to
> counteract the feeling of inferiority and shyness he had
> felt on being treated as a Jew at Princeton.
>
> (See QUOTATIONS, p. 45)

The novel begins with Jake Barnes, the novel's narrator and protag-onist, describing Robert Cohn. Cohn was born to a wealthy Jewish family in New York. At Princeton, Cohn faced rampant anti-Semitism. To minimize his feelings of inferiority and to combat his shyness, he threw himself into boxing, becoming the university's middleweight champion. He married very soon after his graduation, on the rebound from his unhappy college experience. He and his wife had three children. Cohn lost most of his fifty-thousand-dollar inheritance, and, after five years, his wife left him, just when he had made up his mind to walk out on her. After the divorce, Cohn moved to California. There, he began spending time with a literary crowd, and he soon began backing a magazine. While in California, Cohn became involved with Frances Clyne, a manipulative status-seeker. When Cohn's magazine failed, Frances persuaded Cohn to take her to Paris to join the postwar crowd of expatriates.

During his time in Paris, Cohn has few friends, one of whom is Jake. Cohn takes up writing while in Paris, and finishes a novel. As Frances begins to age and starts to lose her beauty, her attitude toward Cohn changes from one of careless manipulation to fierce determination to make him marry her. Jake first becomes aware of Frances's attitude while he dines one night with her and Cohn. Cohn suggests that he and Jake take a weekend trip. Jake suggests that they go to Strasbourg, in northeastern France, because he knows a girl there who can show them around. Cohn kicks him under the table several times before Jake gets the hint and notices Frances's look of displeasure. After dinner, Cohn follows Jake to ask why he mentioned the girl and explains that Frances will not permit him to take any trip that involves seeing a girl.

Summary: Chapter II

> Nobody ever lives their life all the way up except bullfighters.
>
> (See Quotations, p. 45)

That winter, Cohn travels to New York to find a publisher for his novel. There he gains new confidence. The publishers praise the novel, and several women are "nice" to him. He also wins several hundred dollars playing bridge. This success, combined with reading a romantic chronicle of an English gentlemen traveling abroad, infects Cohn with wanderlust. Upon returning to Paris, he comes to Jake's office to persuade him to travel to South America with him, offering to pay for the entire trip. He worries that he is not living life to the fullest. Jake responds that only bullfighters live their lives "all the way up."

Tired of Cohn pestering him in the office, Jake invites Cohn downstairs to have a drink. Jake knows that once they finish the drink it will be easier to get rid of Cohn. At the bar, Cohn continues to harangue Jake about traveling outside of Paris. He complains that he is tired of Paris and the Latin Quarter. Jake asserts that Cohn's discontent has nothing to do with geography, saying, "You can't get away from yourself by moving from one place to another." After the drink, Jake says he needs to return to the office to work. Cohn asks if he can sit outside in the waiting room. Jake allows him to, and, after he is finished at work, he and Cohn have a drink and watch the evening Parisian crowd.

> You can't get away from yourself by moving from one place to another.
>
> *(See* QUOTATIONS, *p. 46)*

ANALYSIS: CHAPTERS I–II

That Jake begins his story by talking about someone else—Robert Cohn—reveals his observer mentality. Jake frequently chooses to speak about other people rather than himself. Often the only means of gaining insight into his character is to read his reactions to other characters. In typical fashion, his portrait of Cohn indirectly reveals aspects of Jake's personality that he does not mention straight out. He states that he likes Cohn, but his description of Cohn has a patronizing tone. He describes Cohn's confrontation with the anti-Semitic atmosphere at Princeton, but his sympathy is tainted with a trivializing attitude, perhaps pointing to a latent anti-Semitism of his own. Hence, we learn that Jake does not respect Cohn. He regards him as a somewhat pathetic, ignorant, and inexperienced man. Jake's disdainful attitude toward Cohn may stem from the fact that Cohn never fought in World War I. Jake also characterizes Cohn as shy and insecure and subject to the control and manipulation of women. This characterization of Cohn as weak reveals Jake's unspoken anxiety regarding his own masculinity.

Cohn worries that he is not living his life the way he ought, but he cannot figure out what is lacking in his life. Like many characters in the novel, he fixates on travel as a solution to his feelings of discontent. Jake, however, realizes that Cohn's unhappiness stems from his personality and lifestyle, and that these will hound him wherever he goes. Cohn's travels, Jake understands, would be as aimless and unfulfilling as his life in Paris. Typically, however, Jake offers no alternative solution to Cohn's dissatisfaction. Instead, he asserts that only bullfighters live their lives to the fullest. He implies that nearly everyone suffers from Cohn's feeling of discontentment, and that Cohn must learn to live with it. Throughout the novel, Jake demonstrates an ability to identify problems but an inability to solve them.

Jake's dinner with Cohn and Frances establishes the novel's recurrent motif of a controlling female overpowering a weak male. Although Cohn may want to go to Strasbourg, he refuses Jake's offer because it would make Frances uncomfortable if he spent time with another woman. Frances controls Cohn and his movements, and he does not, or cannot, stand up to her. This pattern of a strong woman dominating a weak man appears as part of the novel's broad theme of weakened masculinity, which Hemingway explores throughout *The Sun Also Rises*.

Finally, these chapters offer the first introduction to Hemingway's sparse and unadorned prose style. Hemingway rarely uses metaphors or similes to communicate the action of the novel. Instead, he relies on direct, short, simple sentences. His dialogue is brief as well. Characters seldom speak more than a sentence or two at a time. Yet this seemingly minimalist style expresses much through implication and suggestion. We can infer much about Jake, for example, through his descriptions of other people. The details Hemingway chooses to include, although few, are invariably quite revealing.

CHAPTERS III–IV

SUMMARY: CHAPTER III
After Cohn leaves, Jake continues to sit in the café. He catches the eye of a pretty prostitute named Georgette. They have a drink together, and Jake decides it would be nice to have dinner with someone. They catch a horse cab to find a restaurant. While in the cab, Georgette makes a pass at Jake. Jake refuses her, saying he is sick. At dinner he explains that he received a wound in the war that makes such sexual dalliances impossible for him. Georgette exclaims against "that dirty war," but Jake is in no mood to talk about it. He escapes from the conversation when a group of his friends—Cohn and Frances among them—hails him from a nearby table. They invite him and Georgette to go dancing.

The club is hot and crowded. Lady Brett Ashley arrives with a crowd of callow young men wearing jerseys. Jake reacts with hostility to Brett's male friends. Brett states that she can "safely" get drunk around these friends. Jake states that one of these men dances "big-hippily." He says that he knows he should be "tolerant" but that he cannot help being "disgusted"—the implication is that these men are homosexuals. Cohn asks Jake to go for a drink, and Brett joins them. Cohn immediately becomes infatuated with her, and he tries unsuccessfully to persuade her to dance with him. Jake and Brett leave the club together. Before he goes, Jake leaves fifty francs with the club patronne, or owner, telling him to give it to Georgette if she asks for him. Once she and Jake get into a taxi, Brett declares that she is miserable.

SUMMARY: CHAPTER IV

As they ride through the streets of Paris in the taxi, Jake kisses Brett, but she tells him to stop. They love one another, but Brett refuses to have a romantic relationship because Jake cannot have sex. Brett laments their fate, saying that she is now paying for all the "hell" she has made men endure. Jake disingenuously remarks that he finds his war wound funny and rarely thinks about it. As they head to a café to drink, Brett asks Jake to kiss her once more before they arrive. At the café, Jake and Brett again run into their friends. A man called Zizi introduces them to Count Mippipopolous, a Greek man who takes an immediate interest in Brett. Jake and Brett make an appointment to meet the next day, and Jake leaves to return home for the night.

Jake arrives at home, takes his mail from the concierge, and goes to his room. When he gets into bed, he begins to think about his wound. He received it while flying a mission on a "joke front" in Italy. Other people make more of a fuss out of it than he does. He remembers a colonel who visited him in the hospital and said that Jake had "given more than his life." He supposes he would never have had any trouble if he had never met Brett. He begins to cry before drifting off to sleep. After four in the morning, Brett wakes him up by making a drunken scene trying to get past the concierge. The count is waiting outside in his car. Jake lets her up to his room, and Brett reports that the count offered her ten thousand dollars to go to Biarritz, on the southern coast of France, with him, but she turned him down. She wants Jake to go out with them, but he declines. He tries to persuade her to stay, kissing her, but she refuses.

ANALYSIS: CHAPTERS III–IV

In his narration, Jake never directly refers to the aimlessness and purposelessness of his own life and the lives of his friends, but he often implies it. Though he never states that he and his friends suffer from a lack of meaning in their lives, he reveals the absence of meaning through his descriptions of their activities. All the conversations he repeats are full of trite expressions; he and Georgette, for example, agree that the war was a "calamity for civilization," and Jake remarks that they come dangerously close to agreeing that it "would have best been avoided"—a comment that marks the very height of banality. Georgette and Frances talk about whether Paris is clean or dirty and whether it is pleasant or unpleasant. Jake and his friends allfollow the same schedule: wake up, work for a few hours, have lunch, drink, meet a friend, drink, go to a café, drink, go to a club, drink, go home, drink, go to sleep. They are constantly moving from one place to another in an endless procession of social appointments, always drinking copious amounts of alcohol, seemingly never having conversations of any substance. In short, they live a decadent lifestyle devoid of meaning, direction, and emotional connection. Jake's trite conversation with Georgette about the war reveals the extent to which the struggle to cope with the terrible conflict lies at the heart of the Lost Generation's search for meaning. Members of this generation cannot really express what the war has done to them, which stifles them emotionally and psychologically.

When we learn about the mysterious wound that has rendered Jake incapable of having sex but still capable of experiencing sexual desire, his anxiety regarding his masculinity becomes more urgent. His impotence symbolizes the emasculation of World War I veterans. Soldiers suffering from shell shock were considered effeminate and weak. The horrific conditions of trench warfare shattered prewar notions of masculinity, as stoic courage under fire was hardly possible in the trenches. Moreover, the war often involved sitting helplessly under enemy bombardment. This powerless state hardly conformed to the prewar ideal of the tough, masculine soldier who fights with courage to perform his duty. Jake and other soldiers like him were confronted with the task of redefining their masculinity, and Jake's anxiety reveals that he has been unsuccessful so far in this regard.

Brett's mention of getting "safely" drunk with the male friends she brings in and Jake's response that he is "disgusted" by them are coded references to homosexuality. This disgust further demonstrates Jake's anxiety regarding his masculinity. Moreover, we can infer from Brett's actions that her definition of romance requires sex with penetration. Because Jake can never satisfy Brett's sexual desires—she is clearly unsatisfied by or unwilling to consider alternative forms of sexual pleasure—her presence constantly reminds him of his impotence. Jake's mocking reaction to Cohn's interest in Brett also reveals that Cohn's ability to consummate his desire for Brett makes Jake anxious about his own masculinity.

CHAPTERS V–VII

SUMMARY: CHAPTER V

Cohn meets Jake at his office to have lunch. Cohn asks about Brett, and Jake says that she is a drunk and that she is going to marry Mike Campbell, a Scotsman who will be rich someday. Jake also says that Brett's true love died of dysentery during the war. Jake explains that he met Brett while she worked as a V.A.D. (Volunteer Aid Detachment) in the hospital where he was taken for his injury. Cohn gets annoyed that Jake doesn't describe Brett in positive terms; Jake tells Cohn to go to hell. Cohn gets angry at this insult and threatens to leave lunch. Jake smoothes things over and persuades Cohn to stay. Afterward, Jake perceives that Cohn wishes to talk about Brett but avoids bringing up the subject again.

SUMMARY: CHAPTER VI

That evening, Jake goes to meet Brett, but she stands him up. After looking for her in a few places, Jake wanders through the streets of Paris and runs into his friend Harvey Stone, a compulsive gambler. Harvey is broke and claims he has not eaten in days. Jake gives him money. They happen upon Cohn, who is waiting to meet Frances. Harvey insults Cohn, calling him a moron, before leaving to eat. When Frances arrives, she asks to speak to Jake privately. She tells him that Cohn has refused to marry her and that she fears that no man will marry her now. Jake tries to remain neutral. Frances says that she will not receive alimony from her husband because she got divorced in the quickest way; adding to her woes, no one will publish her writing. Trying to remain bright and cheery, she suggests that they rejoin Cohn. In front of Cohn, she tells Jake that Cohn has paid her two hundred pounds to go to England but that she had to wrangle it out of him. In a falsely cheerful manner, she bitterly describes the unpleasant visits to "friends" in England she will have to make, just so Cohn can get rid of her in an orderly manner. She claims that Cohn won't marry her because he wants to tell people that he once had a mistress. Cohn sits through her barrage. Jake excuses himself and leaves them alone.

SUMMARY: CHAPTER VII

> *Couldn't we live together, Brett? Couldn't we just*
> *live together?*
>
> *(See QUOTATIONS, p. 46)*

Jake returns home, and Brett and Count Mippipopolous show up. Jake asks why she missed their appointment but does not believe her when she says she forgot it out of drunkenness. Brett offers to send the count away. Jake tells her not to, but she sends him for champagne. Jake asks why they cannot live together, and she tells him that she would only make him unhappy by cheating on him. She announces that she is leaving Paris for San Sebastian, in Spain, because it will be better for both of them.

The count returns with the champagne, and he begins to describe his philosophy of life. He has been in seven wars and four revolutions. Because he has lived so much, he says, he is able to enjoy everything fully. He thinks the secret to living is to get to know the right values. He is always in love because his values include love. The three of them have a pleasant dinner before going out to a club. The count asks why Brett and Jake do not get married, and they offer curt, false answers. Brett begins to feel miserable and wants to leave. Jake accompanies Brett to her hotel; she does not want him to come up to her room, however. They kiss several times before she pushes him away.

ANALYSIS: CHAPTERS V–VII

What Jake actually says, both as a narrator and as a character, differs sharply from what we can infer about what he actually thinks. The conversation at his lunch with Cohn demonstrates this difference. Jake tells Cohn not to believe him when he says nasty things, but in fact these vicious comments are frequently Jake's most honest expressions of his thoughts and feelings. Very often he hides how he feels, expressing emotion only indirectly within his narration. Harvey Stone stands in stark contrast to Jake. Harvey is totally blunt. For example, he tells Cohn that he considers him a moron and then walks away. Jake does not like Cohn very much either—he even says that he hates him. But he hides this hatred to the point that Cohn considers him his best friend. As with his conversation with Georgette about the war, Jake seems disinclined to communicate openly with other people—even the reader.

Frances and Cohn's messy breakup reveals how little true affection ever existed between them. Cohn abandons Frances as soon as he gains the confidence to do so and finds a woman who interests him more, namely Brett. Frances's main complaint is that she is now too old to find a husband and has wasted her time pursuing Cohn. She is not so much concerned with losing Cohn as with losing the chance to marry. Among Jake and his friends, there are almost no healthy, loving relationships between men and women. Although Jake and Brett seem to truly love one another, Brett is unwilling to commit to Jake. Moreover, she frequently exploits Jake's love for her. She often goes to him for emotional support and then abandons him to pursue affairs with other men, as when, directly after unloading her emotional troubles on Jake, she breaks her appointment with him to spend more time carousing with the count. Although her ill treatment causes Jake pain, he never mentions it to her and only rarely acknowledges it to himself. He essentially allows himself to be abused, unable to stand up to Brett. Ironically, in this respect Jake resembles Cohn, who stoically endures Frances's verbal assaults.

Brett's frequent sexual affairs have clearly not filled the emotional void in her life, a void created, perhaps, by the death of her "true love" during the war. She wanders aimlessly from man to man, just as she wanders from bar to bar. She idealizes the relationship she "would have had" with Jake. For her, Jake represents the unattainable thing that would fulfill her. Hence, she too is a victim of the Lost Generation's inescapable dissatisfaction with life.

Although Brett insists to Jake that the count is "one of us," the count actually serves as a foil for Jake's crowd of restless, dissatisfied, pleasure-seeking friends. He is older and more experienced than they are, and, unlike them, he is confident in his masculinity. Most important, although he has taken part in seven wars and four revolutions, he does not seem to suffer from the empty cynicism that afflicts Jake and his friends. Indeed, more than any other character in the novel, he seems to take genuine pleasure in life. He makes an effort to appreciate the enjoyment that life offers. He urges Brett to drink the champagne slowly, to enjoy it instead of gulping it down. He believes in love, but not in Cohn's excessively romantic, unrealistic brand of love. Thus, love and alcohol, which are so trouble-some for Jake and his friends, are sources of satisfaction for Count Mippipopolous. Learning the value of things for him means under-standing and delighting in what is truly valuable.

CHAPTERS VIII–X

SUMMARY: CHAPTER VIII
Jake does not see Brett or Cohn for a while. He receives a brief card from Brett, who is vacationing in San Sebastian. He also receives a note from Cohn reporting that he has left Paris for the countryside. Frances has left for England. Jake's friend Bill Gorton, an American veteran, arrives from the States. He and Jake plan on going to Spain in order to fish and to attend the fiesta at Pamplona. Bill visits Jake before leaving to visit Budapest and Vienna. When he returns, he tells Jake that he was too drunk to remember very much of his four days in Vienna. While Jake and Bill look for a restaurant, they see Brett get out of a cab. Jake, up to this point, is unaware that she has returned from San Sebastian.

Jake, Bill, and Brett go for drinks together. Brett eventually leaves to meet Mike Campbell, and Jake and Bill eat dinner and drink some more in a restaurant packed with American tourists. Later, they meet Brett and Mike at a café. Mike is drunk and continually men-tions how beautiful Brett is. He wants to return to their hotel early. Jake and Bill decide to attend a boxing match, leaving them alone.

SUMMARY: CHAPTER IX
The next morning, Jake receives a wire from Cohn asking to meet Bill and Jake when they go fishing in Spain. Jake makes the neces-sary arrangements. That evening Jake finds Brett and Mike at a bar. They ask if they may join him in Spain as well. Jake politely responds that they may. When Mike leaves to get a haircut, Brett asks if Cohn will be going to Spain as well. When Jake tells her that he will, she wonders if it will be too "rough" on Cohn. Jake does not understand until she reveals that she was with Cohn in San Sebas-tian. Jake and Brett exchange tense words before eventually decid-ing that Brett should write Cohn, telling him she will be in Spain. To their surprise, when Cohn receives her note, he still wants to go. Jake plans to meet Mike and Brett in Pamplona. Bill and Jake board a train from Paris to Bayonne, where they plan to meet Cohn. The train is overrun with people (whom Jake identifies as Catholics),

and the two men must wait to eat their lunch. When they arrive in Bayonne, Cohn is waiting at the station.

SUMMARY: CHAPTER X

Bill, Jake, and Cohn hire a car to Pamplona. Cohn is nervous because he does not know if Bill and Jake know about his fling with Brett in San Sebastian. He does not believe Brett and Mike will arrive later that night. His "air of superior knowledge" irritates Bill and Jake. In anger, Bill foolishly wagers a hundred pesetas that they will arrive on time. Bill tells Jake that he can't stand it when Cohn gets "superior and Jewish." When Jake picks up his bullfighting tickets, he stops at the cathedral to pray, but he finds his mind wandering.

Jake goes with Cohn to the station to meet Mike and Brett, simply to irritate Cohn. However, Mike and Brett are not on the train, so Jake and Cohn return to the hotel. Jake receives a telegram from Brett and Mike telling him that they have stopped in San Sebastian because Brett is sick. He does not hand the telegram over because he wants to annoy Cohn further, but he does tell Bill and Cohn that Brett and Mike are still in San Sebastian. Bill and Jake plan to take a bus to a small town called Burguete to go fishing, but Cohn decides to stay behind and wait for Brett and Mike. He admits to Jake that he wrote to Brett suggesting a meeting in San Sebastian. When Jake is alone with Bill, Bill reports that Cohn confided in him about his "date" with Brett. Bill says that he thinks Cohn is nice but "so awful."

ANALYSIS: CHAPTERS VIII–X

Bill Gorton provides an important contrast to Jake. While Jake is generally tight-lipped and hesitates to express what is on his mind, Bill takes a different approach to communicating his feelings: he jokes constantly, using humor as a coping mechanism. Bill, like all of Jake's friends, wrestles with the demons of the postwar world. Thus, he feels compelled to drink himself blind for four days in Vienna. But humor allows him to talk about the issues that haunt him in the wake of the Great War. For instance, he addresses the issue of weakened masculinity in the postwar world through his motto of "Never be daunted." He presents this phrase in the context of drinking, telling Jake not to be daunted by how much he needs to drink in order to "catch up." The phrase implicitly touches upon notions of valor and bravery. Bill subtly suggests that in the postwar world, such notions have meaning only in the realm of alcohol.

Jake and Bill are bothered by the Catholics on the train because the Catholics possess strong faith and a belief in God and in moral order. Bill and Jake, on the other hand, lack this confident, secure faith. They struggle with the lack of meaning in their lives. Bill, in particular, seems threatened by the Catholics, joking that their monopolization of the dining car is "enough to make a man join the Klan." Ironically, we learn that Jake is himself Catholic, although he is somewhat reticent about the fact. He periodically looks for solace in his religion, but his faith is not sufficient to anchor him mentally and spiritually. When he goes into church to pray, for example, he finds his mind wandering.

Jake and Bill are hostile to Cohn after his dalliance with Brett. Jake, of course, is painfully jealous of Cohn, and we can infer that Bill picks up on his friend's jealousy and sympathizes with him. But while Jake has had to tolerate Brett's other men before, Cohn is doubly infuriating to Jake because he does not seem to understand that his affair with Brett is over. Cohn is blind to the unspoken rules by which Brett, Jake, and their friends live their lives, and since he knows nothing about Brett's real love for Jake, it is unsurprising that Jake should now find Cohn intensely irritating. Of course, neither Jake nor Bill discusses these feelings directly. Instead, they increasingly express their feelings through anti-Semitic jibes, alluding to Cohn's status as an outsider because he is a Jew and because he is not a veteran of World War I.

Cohn certainly makes a convenient target for contempt. The way he pines for Brett when he clearly should give up is quite pathetic. He is awkward socially and a little slow intellectually at times. Bill and Jake avoid confronting their own shortcomings by mocking Cohn's. Jake seems somewhat more aware that their contempt for Cohn functions as a way to avoid confronting their contempt for themselves. He knows that his petty vengefulness toward Cohn arises from his jealousy of Cohn's relationship with Brett. He yearns for her just as much as Cohn does. But, though he knows that his contemptuous stance toward Cohn displaces his contempt for himself, Jake still treats Cohn poorly.

CHAPTERS XI–XII

SUMMARY: CHAPTER XI

Bill and Jake board a crowded bus to ride to the small, rural town of Burguete. The bus is filled with Basque peasants (who inhabit a region shared by France and Spain in the Pyrenees Mountains). The Basques drink wine from wineskins. They offer their skins to Bill and Jake, who in turn share their bottles of wine. The Spanish countryside is beautiful, and it is cool on top of the bus where Bill and Jake sit. The Basques teach them the proper way to drink from a wine-bag. When the bus stops, Bill and Jake buy some drinks. Some Basque passengers buy them more drinks. Once the bus starts again, an English-speaking Basque engages the two men in friendly conversation. When they arrive in Burguete, the fat innkeeper charges them a high price for their room because it is "the big season." It turns out that Bill and Jake are the only people in the hotel. When they learn that the wine is included, they drink several bottles. Jake goes to bed, musing, "It felt good to be warm and in bed."

SUMMARY: CHAPTER XII

Jake wakes up early, dresses, and goes outside. He digs for worms down beside the stream and collects two tobacco tins full. When Jake goes back inside, Bill begins to joke about irony and pity. He encourages Jake to say only things that are ironic or pitiful. Bill says that Jake doesn't know about how popular irony and pity are because he is an expatriate. He teases that expatriates are drunks who are obsessed with sex and who write nothing worth publishing. Bill says that some people think women support Jake while others think that he is impotent. Jake replies that he is not impotent, that he had an accident. They trade jokes about another man who suffered an accident with similar consequences on horseback, although the story in America is that it was a bicycle accident. Bill declares that he is fonder of Jake than anyone on earth. He states that he could not make this claim in New York because he would sound like a "faggot." He makes an extended joke about how the Civil War was all about homosexuality. "Sex explains it all," he says.

Bill and Jake pack a lunch and bottles of wine, and head to the river. They walk through beautiful meadows, fields, and woods, and, after a long hike, arrive at the river. They place the wine in a spring up the road in order to chill it. Jake fishes with worms, but Bill tries fly-fishing. They both catch many fish, but Bill's fish are bigger. Over their lunch, they joke about the friends they met in the war. Bill then asks Jake if he was ever in love with Brett, and Jake says that he was "for a hell of a long time." They take a nap under the trees and then head back to the inn. They spend five days in Burguete, fishing, eating, drinking, and playing cards. They get no word from Cohn, Brett, or Mike.

ANALYSIS: CHAPTERS XI–XII

Bill and Jake's fishing trip is a calm, beautiful experience, and a nice respite from the disenchantment present throughout much of the novel. The aimless, cynical decadence that characterizes their other activities is curiously absent during the trip. They drink, but not excessively as they do in Paris. They seem content simply to fish, swim, and relax, and they are able to appreciate the beauty of the scenery around them (something Bill is unable to do on his trip to Vienna). Hemingway was an avid fisher and hunter for his entire life, and his faith in the therapeutic value of nature is evident in his description of this trip. Jake and Bill drop their shallow facades and engage in real male bonding, enjoying an easy camaraderie far removed from the petty backbiting they engage in elsewhere in the novel. Although they silently compete over who can catch more and better fish, the competition is amicable. Moreover, Bill and Jake are more open with one another. Their interactions are full of humor, direct talk, empathy, and mutual respect. Symbolic of the spiritual rest that this trip affords the men is the ease with which Jake is able to discuss his wound with Bill. The wound does not provoke the silence or uneasiness in Jake that it usually does. Bill does not react as though Jake's wound has made him any less a man. Earlier in the novel, Jake explains that when he was recovering in the hospital, one man remarked that Jake had given more than his life in the war—implying that Jake might as well be dead. Bill, on the other hand, does not regard Jake in this way. This acceptance helps Jake come to terms with his wound without having to give up his masculinity in the process.

Bill's extended joke on the theme of sex as an explanation for everything reveals the profound influence that Austrian psychologist Sigmund Freud, the founder of psychoanalysis, had exerted on popular culture. It also reveals a latent anxiety toward homosexuality, as he jokingly explains the Civil War as an expression of repressed homosexual tension. His claim that he could not express his fondness for Jake in New York City because he would mark himself as a "faggot" seems to be an attempt to relieve an unconscious anxiety about his close relationship with Jake.

Bill's anxiety about close male relationships could very well stem from World War I: during the war, soldiers experienced intense intimacy in their relationships with one another. Moreover, these relationships were quite domestic in character. The men constantly worried about obtaining adequate food and clothing for one another and relied on one another for emotional support. The war involved a lot of time huddling close together helplessly in dugouts under enemy bombardment. World War I thus had a feminizing influence on bonds between soldiers. In light of this new kind of closeness, the army was careful to distinguish between what it considered the conventional or acceptable forms of male bonding and the deviant or unacceptable forms. By defining homosexuality as a deviant kind of love, nonsexual but equally intense bonds could be considered acceptable. The domestic intimacy of the foxhole was thus deemed acceptable, so long as it was strictly nonsexual. Anxiety over homosexuality continued into peacetime, and it remained important for veterans to affirm the nonsexual nature of their relationships. Bill's joke about being taken for a "faggot" could be read as just such an affirmation. He wants to underline that fact that though he loves Jake very much, he does not love him sexually.

CHAPTERS XIII–XIV

SUMMARY: CHAPTER XIII

Jake receives a letter from Mike telling him that Brett fainted on the train and that they stayed in San Sebastian for three days and won't arrive in Pamplona until Wednesday. Cohn sends a telegram announcing that he will arrive on Thursday. Bill and Jake reply to Cohn's telegram, stating that they are returning to Pamplona that night (Wednesday). Before leaving Burguete, Bill and Jake bid a fond farewell to Wilson-Harris, a British war veteran whom they call Harris. The three men had bonded quickly, and Harris is unhappy to part with them. Although Jake invites Harris to come to Spain, Harris refuses the offer. The three men share drinks in a pub. Harris gives them both his address, along with a dozen flies, saying, "I only thought if you fished them some time it might remind you of what a good time we had."

When Jake and Bill arrive in Pamplona, the innkeeper, Montoya, informs Jake that his friends have arrived. Montoya regards Jake as a real lover and aficionado of bullfighting, in part because Jake stays in Montoya's hotel every year during the fiesta. Jake and Bill find Brett, Mike, and Cohn in a café. Mike regales them with a war story, relating how he gave away another man's medals, since he had none of his own. Everyone watches the unloading of the bulls. When the shining, muscular beasts charge out of the cages, steers (castrated male bovines) work at calming them so that they do not kill one another. The steers are often gored in the process. Jake tells Brett not to look, but she watches anyway, fascinated. Afterward, they go to a café and get drunk. Mike makes a few cutting remarks about Cohn following Brett around like a steer, referring to the fact that Cohn went to San Sebastian after Bill and Jake left Pamplona. Mike berates Cohn for not knowing when he isn't wanted. Bill leads Cohn away, and things calm down. Mike remarks that Brett has had affairs before, but not with Jews or with men who kept hanging around. The group shares a supper in which copious amounts of wine mask the shared feeling of apprehension.

Summary: Chapter XIV

Jake returns to his room that night very drunk. He hears Brett and Mike laughing as they go to bed. Lying in bed, Jake reflects that women make "swell friends" because a man has to be in love with a woman to be friends with her. He feels as if he has been getting something for nothing in his friendship with Brett but that eventually he will have to suffer for the friendship. He decides that people have to pay for everything that is good in life. "Enjoying living was learning to get your money's worth," he concludes. However, he also thinks that in five years this philosophy will seem as silly and useless as all the other philosophies he has constructed. He struggles too with the question of morality. Though he wishes Mike would not insult Cohn, he admits to himself that he enjoys watching Mike do it. The next few days are quiet, as preparations are made for the fiesta.

Analysis: Chapters XIII–XIV

Jake's departure from Burguete to meet Brett and the others at Pamplona despite his love of fishing demonstrates how his desire for Brett disrupts his normal system of values. His departure also indicates the relative strength of male-female bonds compared to male-male bonds in *The Sun Also Rises*. Although Jake enjoys fishing very much, he does not hesitate to abandon it for Brett—indeed, Jake almost always puts Brett ahead of his own plans and his other relationships. Brett's disruptive influence extends to Mike, whose jealousy easily shatters whatever bonds of friendship—or even mere civility—he might share with Cohn.

Mike's war story demonstrates the need to inject the war with humor. Doing so makes the war experience smaller and more manageable. It distances him from the war's horrors. Mike's war story contains no details of actual combat; it is a silly, peaceful anecdote. The story is indicative of the way he and his friends skirt the edges of their war experience. Mike does not discuss his time in the trenches or the effects of the war on his life. Instead, he tries to contain the war within a funny story that begins and ends in the past.

Competition begins to brew between Mike and Cohn over who has proprietary rights to Brett's body, while hostility between Jake and Mike is strangely absent. As a Jewish nonveteran, Cohn functions as a scapegoat. He becomes the convenient target of everyone's resentment, displacing the threat of resentment among the other characters. No one is willing to be held accountable for his cruelty toward Cohn. Mike, for example, explains and tacitly justifies his boorish behavior without accepting responsibility for it by saying simply, "I was drunk."

The episode of the bulls and the steers holds symbolic resonance. We can interpret Jake as a steer, since he, like the castrated male animals, is impotent. The steers' function of making peace among the bulls resembles Jake's function of keeping peace among his rowdy friends. Furthermore, the bulls and the steers do not form a community until one of the steers is dead. Their community is thus based on death, just as Jake's friends' community is based largely on their shared experience during a horrific war—and on their mutual social sacrificing of Cohn. The many symbolic layers within this brief passage demonstrate the richness of Hemingway's writing. Despite its apparent simplicity, his prose has tremendous depth of meaning.

Jake and his friends regard the booming consumerism of the 1920s with contempt. They dislike the tourists who converge on Europe every summer with their money and their arrogance. However, they are obsessed with money themselves. Jake's reflections on friendship are marred by metaphors of money, such as "something for nothing" and "[t]he bill always came." Moreover, Jake says that really enjoying life is "getting your money's worth." Money has become a substitute for meaning in his generation, replacing emotion as the primary structure of human relationships and endeavors. Jake's musings reflect a rather cynical view of human nature that is part of his general disillusionment.

CHAPTER XV

SUMMARY

That Sunday, July 6, at noon, exploding rockets announce the beginning of the fiesta. The square fills with celebrants shouting and drinking wine, men and children dancing, and musicians playing drums and fifes. Everything becomes unreal during the seven days of nonstop drinking, dancing, and music. As Jake notes, it seems to everyone as though "nothing could have any consequences." By the end of the fiesta, even money loses its value for those spending it. The crowd pulls Jake and his friends into a dancing circle around Brett. Afterward, they rush into a crowded wine shop. Everyone inside is dancing and singing. Brett, wearing a wreath of garlic around her neck, learns to drink from a wineskin. Everyone shares food and wine. Jake ducks out to buy two wineskins. When he returns, he finds that Cohn is missing. None of Jake's friends cares where Cohn is, but Jake goes looking for him. He finds Cohn passed out in the back of the shop. Brett, Jake, Cohn, Bill, and Mike all eat a large dinner. Everyone but Jake stays up all night carousing.

An exploding rocket, announcing the release of the bulls, wakes Jake at six o'clock the next morning. From the balcony, Jake watches the crowd run heatedly with the bulls toward the bullring. During the first bullfight, Mike, Cohn, and Brett sit high up in the amphitheater, but Bill and Jake take seats closer to the action. They warn Brett to look away when the horses are gored. Cohn claims that he worries only about being bored. Bill again complains to Jake about Cohn's "Jewish superiority." Montoya introduces Jake to a promising new bullfighter, Pedro Romero. Romero is nineteen years old and the "best-looking boy" Jake has ever seen.

At the bullfight, Romero dazzles everyone who watches him. "This was a real one," says Jake. Afterward, Brett marvels at Romero's skill. She has watched everything, while Cohn has had difficulty dealing with the spectacle. Mike taunts him mercilessly for his weakness. Brett and Mike sit with Jake during the next bullfight. Romero works close to the bull, wearing him down slowly before he moves in for the kill. His suave and graceful performance delights everyone, including aficionados like Jake and Montoya. He utterly overshadows the other bullfighters, and his bullfighting gives the spectators "real emotion." Mike jokes afterward that Brett is falling in love with Romero, and he asks Jake to tell her that bullfighters

beat their mothers. The following day Romero does not fight, and
there is no bullfight scheduled the day after that. The action of the
fiesta continues unabated, however.

ANALYSIS

The fiesta is a Bacchanalian celebration, complete with Brett playing
a symbolic goddess of sexuality and fertility. The drunken revelry is
clearly meant to contrast with the regulated social atmosphere of
France, especially Paris. For the peasants, the fiesta functions as a
release from the long hours worked during the rest of the year. The
fiesta's ritualistic nature gives it a greater depth of meaning than the
drunken sprees in which Jake and his friends engage. The sensual
dancing celebrates sexuality in a meaningful way in contrast to the
empty, easy sexual liberty of Jake's friends. The fiesta is also relatively unspoiled by the rampant vulgarity of consumerism and tour-
ism: people buying wine do not care how much they must pay for it.
Consumerism does, however, begin to encroach on the fiesta, and
the shop owner gives Jake a cheap price on the wineskins only after
he learns that Jake does not intend to sell them later for a profit.

Hemingway portrays Pedro Romero as beautiful, pure, and
whole. Romero is unique in the novel in that he represents a system
of values unspoiled by the war or by disillusionment. His bullfighting technique is genuine, in contrast to the others' fakery. He truly
works close to the bull while the others only give the appearance of
working close to the bull. Romero's purity clashes sharply with the
shallowness of Jake's generation. Romero is able to create "real
emotion"—something genuine—in those who watch him. Moreover, Romero's profession gives his life meaning, whereas Jake
derives no particular satisfaction from being a journalist nor Cohn
from being an author. But Romero's job as a bullfighter forms the
core of his identity. It gives him a purpose in life that the members of
the Lost Generation painfully lack.

Bullfighting offers symbolic commentary on the relationships
between men and women, which are often like battles. The descriptions of the bullfights are laden with sexual tension. Romero's ele-
gant bullfighting style reads remarkably like a skillful act of
seduction. The sexuality expressed in the descriptions is also
remarkably phallic: either the bull penetrates Romero with his
horns or Romero penetrates the bull with his sword. Bullfighting
also functions as a metaphor for the relationships between Brett and
her friends—Brett seems, in some ways, to be a bullfighter. She

SUMMARY & ANALYSIS

effortlessly manipulates men with her sexuality without ever losing her position of power, and she refuses to be dominated as the property of any one man. Perhaps one reason she is attracted to Romero is that she identifies with what he does in the ring.

Hemingway's description of the bullfight provides another characteristic example of his writing style. His prose in the passage is simple and direct. His sentences are generally short and always uncomplicated. He does not rely on metaphor or simile to describe the action; rather, he reports it (we can see here how his career in journalism influenced his prose style). Hemingway writes about "how close Romero always worked to the bull" and how he "avoided every brusque movement." In such passages, Hemingway describes not only Romero, but also his own writing style. He believed that his stripped-down prose allowed him to get "close" to his subject. He avoids the "brusque movements" of rhetorical flourish or elaborate sentence construction. His writing, like Romero's fighting, is always "straight and pure and natural in line."

CHAPTER XVI

SUMMARY

It rains in the morning, leaving Pamplona foggy and dull. Montoya consults Jake regarding a message from the American ambassador inviting Pedro Romero to dine at the Grand Hotel. He fears that foreigners will corrupt Romero. Jake feels the same way and advises him not to deliver the message. He tells Montoya, "There's one American woman down here now that collects bullfighters." Jake finds his friends eating dinner in the hotel dining room. Romero is there as well, eating dinner with a critic. Jake and Romero discuss bullfighting. Romero is modest but extremely passionate about his work. Brett pesters Jake to introduce their group to Romero, and he agrees to do so. Everyone is quite drunk, and Mike shouts, "Tell him that bulls have no balls!" Brett, however, strikes up a private conversation with the young bullfighter. When Montoya enters the dining room, he sees Romero drinking cognac and talking to Brett. He does not even acknowledge Jake's presence. After Romero leaves, Mike begins to insult Cohn again viciously, shouting at him to go away. Jake thinks Cohn actually enjoys the "drunken heroics" of the whole affair. Jake drags Mike away from the table to prevent a fight.

Hordes of English and American tourists arrive in Pamplona for the last day of the fiesta. Bill and Mike leave to bother the English.

Cohn stays behind, but Brett tells him to get lost because she wants to be alone with Jake. She complains to Jake about Mike's behavior and Cohn's following her around. Jake tries to defend Mike, but she asks him not to make her feel guilty. They go for a walk, and Brett asks Jake if he still loves her. After he affirms that he does, she confesses that she is "mad about the Romero boy." Though she says she feels like a "bitch," she asserts, "I've got to do something I really want to do. I've lost my self-respect." Jake agrees to find Romero with her. They go to a café where Romero is seated with other bull-fighters and fight critics. When Romero comes to their table, Jake invites him to sit down. Romero knows there is a mutual attraction between him and Brett. She reads his palm, and they begin to talk about bullfighting, with Jake translating. Romero says that the bulls are his best friends, and that he always kills his best friends "so they don't kill me." Jake leaves them alone. Romero's bullfighting friends stare at Jake with disapproval as he leaves. When Jake returns to the café, Brett and Romero are gone.

Analysis

Mike's behavior toward Cohn reaches the peak of its brutality in this chapter. He desperately tries to get rid of Cohn and insults Cohn to his face about being Jewish. It is not a coincidence that this nasti-ness occurs at the same time that Brett is flirting with Romero. Mike has understandable anxieties about his relationship with Brett—he sees that she is more interested in Romero than in him. He seems to take out these personal insecurities on Cohn. When he shouts at Cohn, "Why don't you see when you're not wanted?" he does so in order to avoid asking the same question of himself. Mike's behavior is one of many examples of characters attacking Cohn for a weak-ness to which they themselves are subject.

Much of the central conflict in *The Sun Also Rises* has to do with anxieties regarding sex. Relationships between women and men in this novel are riddled with conflict, as is apparent in Brett's quarrels with her various lovers. Jake, Mike, and Cohn all lament their inability to earn a full commitment from her. To varying degrees, all three of them would like to control her. They regard their inability to do so as a failure of their masculinity, which torments them. On the surface, then, it would seem that the men in the novel need Brett far more than she needs them. But the nature of Brett's independence is problematic. Although she does not feel compelled to commit to any one man, she still depends on men. She relies on Jake, for example, to give her emotional support. Also, she says she needs to sleep with Romero in order to boost her "self-respect." Hence, within her sexual liberation there remains a kind of bondage—Brett seems to need men to want her in order to feel good about herself.

Despite this dependence, Brett remains true to herself at all times. Although she feels like a "bitch" for doing so, she generally does whatever she wants. She abandons Jake for Cohn, and later she leaves Mike for Romero. In this carefree indulgence, she contrasts markedly with Jake, who ignores his own feelings and desires whenever they conflict with Brett's requests. He is willing to do anything for her, regardless of the personal cost, and this chapter underscores this weakness. Although he loves Brett, he helps her find Romero so that she can sleep with him. Jake thus utterly betrays his own desires. His blind love for Brett overpowers all of his self-interest.

Jake's love also undermines his values in this chapter. He has genuine passion for bullfighting. When he tells Montoya to discard the note from the American ambassador, Jake demonstrates that he understands and fears the threat foreigners pose to Romero's career. Yet, later the same night, he sets Romero up with Brett. At the opening of the chapter, Jake defends Romero from harmful, outside influences; at the end of the chapter, he pushes Romero toward these same forces. In doing so, he betrays not only the sport he loves but also his friendship with Montoya. Jake's love for Brett is the most powerful, controlling force in his life, and it greatly disrupts everything else that he holds dear.

Chapter XVII

Summary

Jake meets Mike and Bill at a bar. Edna, a friend of Bill, is with them. Mike and Bill have been tossed out of a café for nearly causing a brawl among the English and American tourists. The group goes to another café, where Cohn approaches Jake and demands to know where Brett is. Jake refuses to tell him. Mike says that she has "gone off with the bullfighter chap." Furious, Cohn calls Jake a pimp. Jake takes a swing at Cohn, and a fistfight ensues. Cohn displays his athletic prowess, knocking Mike to the ground and Jake out cold. When Jake comes to, he returns to the hotel. Mike stays at the café with Edna. When Jake arrives back at the hotel, Bill tells him that Cohn wants to see him. Jake finds Cohn lying face down on the bed in tears. He begs Jake to forgive him, but Jake refuses. Cohn says that Jake is the only friend he has, and Jake finally gives in, says he forgives him, and shakes his hand.

In the morning, Jake finds that Bill and Mike have already gone to the stadium. A man is killed during the release of the bulls, gored in the back. The crowds of people ignore his body, running over and around him to reach the stadium. Jake goes to a café, where he talks to a waiter about the dead man. The waiter does not see the sense in bullfighting. A man died, he notes, "All for sport. All for pleasure." Jake goes back to bed, but Bill and Mike knock on the door. Jake learns that Cohn found Brett and Romero together. Cohn apparently hit Romero over and over, but Romero kept getting up and attacking. Finally, Cohn said he would not hit Romero again, and Romero hit him as hard as he could before collapsing. Brett then gave Cohn a tongue-lashing. Cohn tearfully begged Romero to shake hands, but when he offered his hand, Romero hit him again. Later, Mike told Brett how he felt about her affairs with "Jews and bullfighters." She retorted that the British aristocracy has made her miserable. Her husband, Lord Ashley, forced her to sleep on the floor with him and threatened to kill her all the time. He slept with a loaded service revolver, which Brett unloaded every night. As Bill leaves, Jake asks if he has heard about the man that was gored to death. Bill knows nothing about it.

ANALYSIS

Brett acts as something of a femme fatale in this chapter. Whatever her unrestricted sexuality means to her, it clearly functions as a destructive, corrupting influence on men. Because she refuses to confine herself to one man, she becomes a destroyer of men. She is represented as a threat to Romero's purity, and she causes irresolvable tension among Jake and the other men. Every man who desires her suffers from anxiety regarding his masculinity. She, on the other hand, is often described in masculine terms: she wears her hair in a "boyish style," and she often refers to herself as a "chap." Even her name—Brett—is masculine. It is highly probable that Brett's somewhat thoughtless treatment of the men in her life results from her unhappy marriage. Her husband controlled her with threats of murder, so she is careful never to be placed in a submissive, dominated position in her subsequent sexual relationships. She follows her own desires rather than restricting herself to one man.

Cohn, in contrast, represents prewar romantic values. His relationship with Brett corrupts these values. When he physically attacks Mike, Jake, and Romero, he breaks the code of good sportsmanship by fighting outside the gym. When he realizes what he has done, he is disgusted with himself. In trying to defend the prewar, romantic ideal of love, he compromises his prewar value system. It seems also that his relationship with Brett results in his being figuratively castrated. After his series of violent attacks, he is reduced to tearful begging for forgiveness. His desperate pleas "to shake hands" represent his doomed attempt to reclaim the gentlemanly values that he has betrayed. He retreats to an old ritual of good sportsmanship, but it now seems pathetic.

The episode of the man being killed by the bull is charged with symbolic meaning. On one level, it parallels Cohn's plight. His desire and gullibility allow Brett to maim him and leave him to suffer. Just as the crowds do not stop to help the wounded man, neither Jake nor his friends give much thought to Cohn's destruction. Rather, they go on with their incessant drinking and carousing. On a larger level, the death of the wounded man represents the death of Cohn's entire value system. The world, like the crowd, rushes on without these outdated principles, barely aware of their loss.

One could argue that, ultimately, *The Sun Also Rises* is Cohn's story. He is the first character Hemingway introduces, and his presence forms the impetus for the novel's plot. Furthermore, the failure of his value system stands as the novel's climax. Cohn's values are traditional values; he alone among Jake's acquaintances holds onto the outdated, prewar notions of bravery, honesty, and love. When Cohn hits Jake, he betrays these values, and the last vestiges of the prewar world are shattered. The sun has fully set on the past generation's code of belief and conduct. The time for these principles, like Cohn's story, has come to an end.

CHAPTERS XVIII–XIX

SUMMARY: CHAPTER XVIII

Cohn leaves Pamplona. Brett meets everyone else at a café. She reports that Romero looks quite bad after his beating but that he plans to bullfight anyway. Mike sullenly remarks, "Brett's got a bullfighter. She had a Jew named Cohn, but he turned out badly." Brett draws Jake away from the café as Mike overturns the table, dumping beer and food all over the floor.

Brett suggests that they go into a church because she wants to pray for Romero, but she becomes nervous and wants to leave not long after they enter. They return to the hotel. Montoya bows to Jake and Brett but does not smile. Brett retires to Romero's room, and Jake checks on Mike. Mike is languishing on his bed in a drunken stupor, his room a mess. Bill and Jake eat lunch before they meet Brett for the last bullfight.

Romero sends his cape to Brett for her to hold during the fights. Belmonte, one of the three bullfighters, has come out of retirement to fight. His reputation for working dangerously close to the bull is legendary. The crowd thus expects more from him than he could ever achieve, even at the height of his career. The crowd jeers at him and insults him. However, they love Romero's calm, smooth style and natural talent. Romero faces the bull that killed the man running in the street that morning. He leads the bull with a grace that appeals to the crowd. After he kills the bull, its notched ear is cut off. He gives it to Brett. Jake and Bill drink in a café afterward. Jake is depressed, so Bill urges him to drink three absinthes in a row. He finds Mike sitting in his hotel room in the process of getting drunk. Brett has left Pamplona on a train with Romero.

SUMMARY: CHAPTER XIX

> "Oh, Jake . . . we could have had such a damned good
> time together."

(See QUOTATIONS, p. 47)

The next day, Mike, Bill, and Jake share a car to Bayonne. They get drunk and drive to Saint Jean de Luz to drop Mike off. Jake says goodbye to Bill at the train station in Bayonne. Jake spends time making friends in Bayonne by tipping people generously. He takes a morning train to San Sebastian for a few days of relaxation. Not long after his arrival, however, he receives two telegrams, one forwarded from Paris and one forwarded from Pamplona. Both are from Brett. She wants him to come to the Hotel Montana in Madrid because she is "in trouble." He immediately makes arrangements to leave San Sebastian and meet her.

When Jake arrives in Madrid, Brett greets him with a kiss. She has sent Romero away. She sent for Jake because she was not sure if she could make Romero leave, and she did not have money to get away. Romero offered her money, but she would not take it. He was ashamed of her at first and wanted her to grow her hair so she would look more like a woman. He wanted to marry her so that she would never leave him. But she forced Romero to leave because she did not want to ruin him. She adds that she wants to go back to Mike. She and Jake go to a bar and have three martinis each before having lunch in a nice restaurant, where Jake drinks three bottles of wine. He then orders two more bottles of wine and downs a couple of glasses. Brett asks Jake not to get drunk and assures him that he will be "all right." They get a taxi to drive around town. Jake puts his arm around her, and Brett says, "Oh, Jake . . . we could have had such a damned good time together." Jake replies, "Yes, isn't it pretty to think so?"

ANALYSIS: CHAPTERS XVIII–XIX

Belmonte the bullfighter is a symbol of the entire Lost Generation. He has no purpose in his current time and place, and his important accomplishments are behind him. He achieved great fame in his younger days, and many consider him among the greatest bullfighters. When he retired, the legends about his prowess and bravery grew. When he comes out of retirement, however, the same legends work against him. He can never live up to the image that has sprung up around him. Thus, the crowd turns on him, and he becomes bitter and indifferent in the ring. His plight shares many similarities with that of Jake and his circle of friends, people who all seem to be passing time until the ends of their lives rather than living with any sense of purpose. The Lost Generation feels a similar kind of bitterness and indifference for much the same reason—the same cultures and nations its members served in the World War I have now abandoned them.

Brett portrays her split with Romero as a selfless act, stating that their living together was bad for him and his career. Though she asserts that "I'm not going to be one of these bitches that ruins children," there is probably more to their breakup than self-sacrificing benevolence. Brett quickly realizes that Romero wants her to change into a more traditionally feminine woman, growing her hair to be more "womanly." Brett's refusal to consider such conventional changes makes their relationship untenable. She would rather split with Romero than compromise the person she wants to be. Moreover, a central feature of Brett's personality is her inability to settle. Like the lives of all of Jake's friends, Brett's life is characterized by a compulsion to wander aimlessly. It is unlikely that her love for Romero, even if it were genuine, could make her settle down.

Brett and Jake, on the other hand, have a relatively stable relationship. It seems that his impotence makes this stability possible. As a sexual relationship between them is impossible, her sexuality cannot destroy him the way it does other men. Perhaps his love for her is different from the love that other men feel for her by virtue of the impossibility of its consummation. Mike and Cohn's obsession with Brett has very little to do with love for her. Rather, it represents a need to satisfy their lust and to solidify their masculinity through their dominance and ownership of her.

Despite her decision to leave Romero before she corrupts him, Brett seems less changed than Jake does. She still idealizes the relationship they "would have had," stating that they would have had a "wonderful time" together. Jake, on the other hand, expresses doubt, encapsulated in the novel's final line: it is "pretty to think" that they would have had a grand affair if he had been sexually functional, but it is possible that their relationship would have ended as badly as Brett's other sexual relationships. Jake has not stopped suffering because he cannot have Brett, but he seems to have reached a more realistic appreciation of their situation as well as his own.

IMPORTANT QUOTATIONS EXPLAINED

1.   Robert Cohn was once middleweight boxing champion of
     Princeton. Do not think I am very much impressed by that as
     a boxing title, but it meant a lot to Cohn. He cared nothing
     for boxing, in fact he disliked it, but he learned it painfully
     and thoroughly to counteract the feeling of inferiority and
     shyness he had felt on being treated as a Jew at Princeton.

These lines open the novel, as Jake begins a brief biographical sketch
of Robert Cohn. This passage presents many of the themes and
motifs that the novel goes on to develop, such as competitiveness
and resentment between men and insecurity. For example, Cohn
suffers from feelings of "inferiority" because he is Jewish, and, as
soon becomes clear, nearly every male character in the novel finds
something about which to feel inferior. It is significant that none of
the themes in this brief passage is presented directly; rather, they are
all invoked implicitly, demonstrating Hemingway's style of stating
relatively little but implying a great deal.

These sentences also have a noticeable tone of condescension. As
the novel progresses, this condescension develops into outright hostility and antagonism toward Cohn. Over the course of the novel,
we come to realize that Jake's hostile and skeptical attitude toward
Cohn is bound up with jealousies and insecurities of his own.

Finally, we learn from this passage that Cohn has an intense need
to be accepted. Although he dislikes boxing, he perfects it in order to
better his social position at Princeton. This need for acceptance
proves harmful to Cohn in his relationships with Jake and Brett,
who cannot stomach his insecurities.

2.   [Cohn:] "I can't stand it to think my life is going so fast and
     I'm not really living it."
     [Jake:] "Nobody ever lives their life all the way up except
     bull-fighters."

In this quotation, taken from Chapter II, Cohn verbalizes one of the
key dilemmas afflicting the Lost Generation. In the wake of World

War I, many young men and women felt their lives had no purpose or substance. Cohn worries that he is wasting his brief time on earth. Jake's comfort is really not comfort at all. He advises Cohn that "[n]obody" feels fulfilled in their lives, except a small group of extraordinary people. Of course, Cohn cannot become a bullfighter. Jake implies that Cohn must learn to live with his feeling of discontent. This advice is demonstrative of Jake's character: although he understands the flaws of the world and the people around him, he almost never takes action to correct those flaws. He simply accepts them, as he advises Cohn to do.

3.   "You can't get away from yourself by moving from one place to another."

Jake says these words to Cohn in Chapter II when Cohn tries to convince him to travel to South America. Cohn feels dissatisfied with his life in Paris, and he believes that a change of location will fill the void he senses in his life. Jake knows that such reasoning is nonsense— Cohn's unhappiness stems from his outdated values and his decadent lifestyle, which will not be any different anywhere else. As with the previous quote, Jake demonstrates a unique insight into the problems and activities of the postwar generation. Many of Jake's friends, and indeed Jake himself, try to cure their unhappiness through constant travel, either on a small scale, from bar to bar, or on a large one, from country to country. Jake shows here that he knows that such travel is futile and ultimately purposeless. The discontent of the Lost Generation is psychological, not geographic.

4.   [Jake:] "Couldn't we live together, Brett? Couldn't we just live together?"
[Brett:] "I don't think so. I'd just tromper you with everybody."

This exchange between Jake and Brett, which occurs in Chapter VII, after Brett shows up at Jake's home in Paris with Count Mippi-popolous, encapsulates the central conflict of the novel, which is rarely directly expressed. One must read closely to understand what is at stake and what is being discussed. As always in Hemingway's prose, while little is said, much is communicated. Jake begs Brett to be with him, but she replies that she would always *"tromper"* him, a French word here meaning "to commit adultery." A wound Jake received during the war rendered him impotent, and he thus cannot satisfy Brett's need for sex. With her words, she is telling Jake that she would have to go with other men behind Jake's back, which she knows he wouldn't be able to stand. This central, intractable emotional conflict forms the backdrop for the action of the novel.

5. "Oh, Jake," Brett said, "we could have had such a damned good time together."

 Ahead was a mounted policeman in khaki directing traffic. He raised his baton. The car slowed suddenly pressing Brett against me.

 "Yes," I said. "Isn't it pretty to think so?"

These are the final lines of the novel, presenting Brett and Jake's final dialogue, spoken in a taxi at the end of Chapter XIX. Jake has endured an attack by Cohn and helped Brett in her seduction of Romero. Brett has pushed Romero away and now finds herself alone again. In this concluding passage, the lament over what could have been is truly poignant, and for many this represents the novel's finest moment. Just as Brett voices, one last time, the dream that the two of them could have had a relationship, a policeman raises his baton and symbolically signals a halt. The car's sudden deceleration presses Brett tantalizingly close to Jake, echoing a number of similar scenes earlier in the novel, but the barrier between them is quite clear now. Moreover, Jake's slightly cynical and bitter reply shows that he has no illusions about their relationship. He seems to appreciate the fact that a relationship between himself and Brett, if such a thing had been possible, would have been unlikely to end differently than any of her other failed relationships. Yet Jake's subtle doubts only increase the poignancy of the novel's closing lines. Their relationship is revealed to have been merely a beautiful dream, a dream that is now slipping away forever.

KEY FACTS

FULL TITLE
The Sun Also Rises

AUTHOR
Ernest Hemingway

TYPE OF WORK
Novel

GENRE
Modernist novel; travelogue; novel of disillusionment

LANGUAGE
English

TIME AND PLACE WRITTEN
Mid-1920s, Paris

DATE OF FIRST PUBLICATION
1926

PUBLISHER
Charles Scribner's Sons

NARRATOR
Jake Barnes

POINT OF VIEW
Jake tells the entire story from his own point of view.

TONE
Somber, detached, ironic, nostalgic

TENSE
Past

SETTING (TIME)
1924

SETTING (PLACE)
The novel begins in Paris, France, moves to Pamplona, Spain, and concludes in Madrid, Spain.

PROTAGONIST
Jake

MAJOR CONFLICT
Jake is in love with Lady Brett Ashley, but they cannot maintain a relationship because he was rendered impotent by a war wound. Jake loses numerous friendships and has his life repeatedly disrupted because of his loyalty to Brett, who has a destructive series of love affairs with other men.

RISING ACTION
Jake, Brett, and their friends pursue a dissipated life in Paris; Jake introduces Brett to Robert Cohn; Brett and Cohn have an affair; Cohn follows Brett to Pamplona.

CLIMAX
The jilted Cohn beats up Mike and Jake, and afterward Pedro Romero.

FALLING ACTION
Jake and his friends leave Spain; Jake enjoys the solitude of San Sebastian; Brett wires Jake to rescue her in Madrid after forcing Romero to leave her.

THEMES
The aimlessness of the Lost Generation; male insecurity; the destructiveness of sex

MOTIFS
The failure of communication; excessive drinking; false friendships

SYMBOLS
Bullfighting

FORESHADOWING
The behavior of the bulls repeatedly foreshadows the actions of the people in the novel.

KEY FACTS

STUDY QUESTIONS &
ESSAY TOPICS

STUDY QUESTIONS

1. *How does Hemingway show that Jake is insecure about his masculinity early in the novel?*

Jake does not mention his insecurities directly. We must search for information about them in his reactions and descriptions of others. Jake takes a condescending attitude toward Cohn. His descriptions cast Cohn as a weak, inexperienced man. Jake's contempt seems to arise partly from Cohn's feminized status. He characterizes Cohn as timid and easily controlled by a strong woman like Frances. This emphasis on Cohn's lack of masculinity can be seen as a reflection of Jake's own insecurities about his manhood. Also, Jake resents the group of male friends with whom Brett dances at the club. His statements about them subtly imply that they are homosexuals. Brett can "safely" get drunk around them, for instance, because they have no interest in having sex with her. Jake realizes that he should be "tolerant," but admits that he is in fact "disgusted" by them. His irrational disgust likely stems from his perception of them as unmanly, illustrating his worries about his own manliness. Thus, Hemingway uses Jake's contempt for Cohn's feeble masculinity and his reaction of abhorrence toward Brett's homosexual friends to reveal his anxiety about his own masculinity.

2. *Compare Jake's relationship to Brett with Cohn's relationship to Frances.*

Jake adopts a patronizing attitude toward Cohn, especially when he describes Cohn's interactions with women. Early in the novel, Frances dominates Cohn, and her wishes overrule his. Because of Frances's domination of Cohn, Jake seems to lack respect for him. But Jake's relationship with Brett is actually quite similar to that between Cohn and Frances. Jake is willing to do anything for Brett. He allows her to lean on him for emotional support and then abandon him for other men. He even helps facilitate her affair with Pedro Romero. Cohn eventually breaks with Frances; despite her verbal abuse, he is able to end his relationship with her. Jake, on the other hand, is too attached to Brett to ever let go of her, despite her mistreatment of him. Thus, in some ways, Cohn is stronger in his relationship with Frances than Jake is in his with Brett.

3.   *How is Count Mippipopolous like Jake and his friends? How is he different?*

Like Jake and his friends, the count has seen a great deal of violence. He has survived seven wars and four revolutions. He is also an expatriate, a Greek man living abroad. Furthermore, he loves to seek pleasure, as do Jake and his friends. However, unlike the members of the Lost Generation, he seems to genuinely enjoy these pleasures. Jake and his friends are all engaged in an attempt to forget the war and their unhappiness by drinking themselves into oblivion while filling their spare time with social appointments. The count, on the other hand, delights in food, wine, and spending time with friends. These things satisfy him and make him happy. He covets Brett, but this desire does not torment him as it does Jake, Cohn, and Mike. He is content to enjoy her company when he can. Thus, while the count has essentially the same lifestyle as Jake and his friends, he derives joy from it while they do not, and he is not a victim of their disillusioned cynicism.

SUGGESTED ESSAY TOPICS

1. *Compare Jake and Cohn. How does the fact that Jake went to war and Cohn did not make them different from each other? What qualities do they share with the rest of their acquaintances? Is it safe to call them both outsiders?*

2. *Bill tells Jake that "[s]ex explains it all." To what extent is Bill's statement true of the novel* The Sun Also Rises?

3. *Discuss the characterization of Lady Brett Ashley. Is she a sympathetic character? Is she a positive female role model? Does she treat her male friends cruelly?*

4. *Read closely and analyze one of the longer passages in which Hemingway describes bulls or bullfighting. What sort of language does Hemingway use? Does the passage have symbolic possibilities? If the bullfighting passages do not advance the plot, how do they function to develop themes and motifs?*

5. *Analyze the novel in the context of World War I. How does the experience of war shape the characters and their behavior? Examine the differences between the veterans, like Jake and Bill, and the nonveterans, like Cohn and Romero.*

6. *Why is Cohn verbally abused so often in the novel? Is it because he is Jewish? Why does Mike attack Cohn but not Jake, whom Brett actually loves? Why does Cohn accept so much abuse?*

7. *Discuss the problem of communication in the novel. Why is it so difficult for the characters to speak frankly and honestly? In what circumstances is it possible for them to speak openly? Are there any characters who say exactly what is on their mind? If so, how are these characters similar to each other?*

REVIEW & RESOURCES

QUIZ

1. In what sport did Robert Cohn participate at Princeton?

   A. Soccer
   B. Golf
   C. Boxing
   D. Track and field

2. Where does the fiesta occur?

   A. Pamplona, Spain
   B. Burguete, Spain
   C. Paris, France
   D. Mexico City, Mexico

3. What is Cohn's profession?

   A. Tennis player
   B. Writer
   C. Shoemaker
   D. He is unemployed

4. In what war was Jake injured?

   A. World War II
   B. Spanish-American War
   C. Persian Gulf War
   D. World War I

5. Who knows the most about bullfighting?

   A. Brett
   B. Jake
   C. Bill Gorton
   D. Cohn

6. What country does Jake come from?

    A. America
    B. Great Britain
    C. France
    D. Canada

7. What is Brett's title?

    A. Lady
    B. Duchess
    C. Princess
    D. Mrs.

8. Who wins the fight between Jake, Mike, and Cohn?

    A. Jake
    B. Mike
    C. They never fight
    D. Cohn

9. What is the name of the owner of the hotel where Jake stays during the fiesta?

    A. Pedro Romero
    B. Montoya
    C. Belmonte
    D. Geoffrey Chaucer

10. Who is Count Mippipopolous?

    A. A man Jake killed during the war
    B. A talented fisherman
    C. A bullfighting expert
    D. A wealthy Greek expatriate living in Paris

11. How does Brett and Romero's relationship end?

    A. Brett walks out on Romero
    B. Romero sleeps with another woman
    C. Brett forces Romero to leave
    D. Jake kills Romero

12. Which of the following characters is physically impotent?

    A.   Robert Cohn
    B.   Jake Barnes
    C.   Bill Gorton
    D.   All of the above

13. In what sport do Jake and Bill engage while in Spain?

    A.   Fishing
    B.   Fox hunting
    C.   Boxing
    D.   Horseshoes

14. Which of the following characters does not want to sleep with Brett?

    A.   Jake Barnes
    B.   Robert Cohn
    C.   Mike Campbell
    D.   They all want to sleep with Brett

15. What does Jake say to Brett at the end of the novel?

    A.   "Things have a funny way of working out"
    B.   "Isn't it pretty to think so?"
    C.   "No, of course I didn't invite him!"
    D.   "I love you."

16. How good a bullfighter is Pedro Romero?

    A.   He is the best around
    B.   He is past his prime
    C.   He works hard but is only mediocre
    D.   He is generally poor but shows flashes of brilliance

17. How does Cohn react to the bullfight?

    A.   He is bored
    B.   He refuses to go to the bullfight
    C.   He loves every second of it
    D.   It makes him sick

REVIEW & RESOURCES

18. Where did Brett and Jake meet?

    A.   On a bus
    B.   At an Alcoholics Anonymous meeting
    C.   At a hospital during World War I
    D.   At the previous year's fiesta

19. Why does Cohn decide not to go fishing?

    A.   He is too hung over to travel
    B.   He can't afford the money for the bus ticket
    C.   He wants to wait for Brett
    D.   Bill and Jake make him feel unwelcome

20. What do most people drink at the fiesta?

    A.   Wine
    B.   Absinthe
    C.   Brandy
    D.   Whiskey

21. Who introduces Brett to Romero?

    A.   Mike
    B.   Montoya
    C.   Cohn
    D.   Jake

22. What interrupts Jake's vacation in San Sebastian in the novel's final chapter?

    A.   A visit from Cohn
    B.   A wire from Brett
    C.   The outbreak of World War II
    D.   The death of Romero

23. What does Cohn ask Romero to do after Cohn beats him up?

    A.   Leave Pamplona
    B.   Never bullfight again
    C.   Shake his hand
    D.   Promise to treat Brett well

24. What is Cohn's girlfriend's name?

   A. Frances
   B. Edna
   C. Georgette
   D. Marie

25. With whom does Brett secretly go to San Sebastian?

   A. Count Mippipopolous
   B. Bill Gorton
   C. Robert Cohn
   D. Montoya

SUGGESTIONS FOR FURTHER READING

ANDERSON, CHARLES R. *Ernest Hemingway: Critiques of Four Major Novels.* Ed. Carlos Baker. New York: Charles Scribner's Sons, 1962.

BENSON, JACKSON J. "Roles and the Masculine Writer." In *Brett Ashley,* edited by Harold Bloom, 76–85. New York: Chelsea House Publishers, 1991.

BURGESS, ANTHONY. *Ernest Hemingway and His World.* New York: Charles Scribner's Sons, 1978.

FARRELL, JAMES T. "The Sun Also Rises." In *Ernest Hemingway: The Man and His Work,* edited by John K. M. McCaffery, 221–225. New York: The World Publishing Company, 1950.

GOODMAN, PAUL. *Ernest Hemingway: Five Decades of Criticism.* Ed. Linda Welshimer Wagner. East Lansing: Michigan State University Press, 1974.

REVIEW & RESOURCES

GURKO, LEO. *Ernest Hemingway and the Pursuit of Heroism.* New York: Thomas Y. Crowell Company, 1968.

VANCE, WILLIAM L. "Implications of Form in *The Sun Also Rises.*" In *The Twenties: Poetry and Prose: Twenty Critical Essays,* edited by Richard E. Langford and William E. Taylor, 87–91. Florida: Everett Edwords Press, 1966.

VOSS, ARTHUR. *The American Short Story: A Critical Survey.* Norman: University of Oklahoma Press, 1973.

WALDHORN, ARTHUR. *A Reader's Guide to Ernest Hemingway.* New York: Farrar, Straus, and Giroux, 1972.